Breakthrough Strategies to TEACH and COUNSEL Troubled Youth

Social Skills • School Skills • Coping Skills LESSON SERIES

Temper and Tantrum Tamers

Ruth Herman Wells, M.S.
Illustrated by Daniel C. Wells

Coping Skills

Dedicated to Chris Wells

© 1993 by Youth Change

ISBN 1-891881-05-1
ISBN 1-891881-15-9 Series

All rights reserved. The lesson plans in this book may not be reproduced in any form or by any means without the prior written permission of the author. The lesson handouts may only be reproduced by the purchaser for use with students during instruction.

YOUTH CHANGE

On-Site • Conference • General Session • Taped WORKSHOPS
Newsletter • Lesson Book INTERVENTION RESOURCES
275 N. Third St., Woodburn, Oregon 97071
1-800-545-5736 • youthchg.com

Resources by This Author:

A Child's Guide to Surviving in a Troubled Family
All The Best Answers for the Worst Problems
All-Time Favorite Lessons
Build On-the-Job Success Skills
Breakthrough Strategies to Teach and Counsel Series
Breakthrough Strategies Workshop on Tape
Coping Skills Sampler
Education: Don't Start the Millennium Without It
Learning to Like the Kid in the Mirror
Ready, Set, Go! for Independent Living
Temper and Tantrum Tamers
The Last Chance School Success Guide
Turn On the Turned-Off Student
What Every Girl Needs to Know About the Real World
The Quickest Kid Fixer-Uppers: Volumes 1-4

Lesson 1

Take the Aggressiveness Truth Test

Goal: To teach students what is aggressive behavior, and to assist aggressive students who deny that they have a problem with aggressiveness, to consider if their behavior is considered aggressive by others.

Materials: Chalkboard, chalk, pens, one copy for each student of the "The Aggressiveness Truth Test."

1. ▲ **Inform** the students that they will be learning about aggressive behavior. **Draw** an outline of a person on the board, and **ask** the students to draw on the outline to illustrate aggressiveness. **Ask** the students to use the phrase "swear words" instead of writing actual profane words. **Discuss** the completed picture with the class, and **note** that now all the students know what aggressiveness is, and can no longer honestly say "I didn't know that behavior was aggressive."

2. ▲ **Ask** the students to discuss where and how children learn aggressiveness and **elicit** answers such as "by watching violent movies" or "from the all the hitting and punching that happens in our neighborhood". **Assist** the class to identify that there are many opportunities to learn aggressive behavior.

   ▲ **Ask** the students to consider how well aggressive conduct works in the activities they are involved with. **Assist** the students to notice that aggressiveness can put them into conflict with community, school and work place rules and laws. **Assist** the class to discuss that although youth can be exposed to a lot of aggressiveness, especially through the media, in the real world aggressiveness can lead to legal, community and school sanctions.

3. ▲ **Ask** the students to discuss if any of the class members have problems with aggressiveness. **Permit** even aggressive students to assert that they do not use aggressive conduct. **Ask** the students to determine if their perceptions are accurate by taking the "The Aggressiveness Truth Test". To take the test, the class must assist each student to identify four adults and four peers who have extensive contact with the student, and would be aware of any aggressive conduct. To complete the test, a student must ask each of the selected adults and peers to honestly complete the test, as directed on the test form. (To best ensure that this test will accurately reflect the student's level of aggressiveness, be sure that many of the adults and peers selected perceive the aggressive student as aggressive, and will reflect this perception on the test.) The completed tests can later be reviewed and discussed by the class, with a focus of beginning to assist the aggressive student to understand that s/he may have a problem with aggressive conduct.

4. ▲ Review the major points of this lesson:
   • **You now clearly know what aggressiveness is, and can no longer honestly say "I didn't know that behavior was aggressiveness."**
   • **There are many opportunities to learn aggressive behavior, but in the real world, aggressiveness can lead to legal, community and school sanctions.**
   • **Although you may not feel that you act aggressively, the peers and adults who have extensive contact with you, may feel that the truth is that you do have problems with aggressive conduct.**

The Aggressiveness Truth Test

Each of the participating adults and peers should write in the small blanks, the number of times, they estimate that they say the following phrases (or similar ones) to you each week. The adults and peers can add into the larger blank spaces, one or more additional phrases they also say to you.

Do Adults Think You are Too Aggressive?
"If you do that again, I'm going to have to send you to the...principal, parole officer, counselor, etc."
    Number of times/week this phrase is said to you by:
    Adult #1: ___   Adult #2 ___   Adult #3 ___   Adult #4 ___

"Unless you stop, I'm going to have to call your...mother, parole officer, counselor, etc."
    Number of times/week this phrase is said to you by:
    Adult #1: ___   Adult #2 ___   Adult #3 ___   Adult #4 ___

"You're going to have to leave if you continue to..."
    Number of times/week this phrase is said to you by:
    Adult #1: ___   Adult #2 ___   Adult #3 ___   Adult #4 ___

"Get your hands off of...that, her, him, them!"
    Number of times/week this phrase is said to you by:
    Adult #1: ___   Adult #2 ___   Adult #3 ___   Adult #4 ___

Adults can insert their own phrase here: _____
    Number of times/week this phrase is said to you by:
    Adult #1: ___   Adult #2 ___   Adult #3 ___   Adult #4 ___

Do Your Peers Think You are Too Aggressive?
"Leave me ALONE!"
    Number of times/week this phrase is said to you by:
    Peer #1: ___   Peer #2 ___   Peer #3 ___   Peer #4 ___

"Get your hands off of my...!!"
    Number of times/week this phrase is said to you by:
    Peer #1: ___   Peer #2 ___   Peer #3 ___   Peer #4 ___

"Stay away from me! You're hurting me!"
    Number of times/week this phrase is said to you by:
    Peer #1: ___   Peer #2 ___   Peer #3 ___   Peer #4 ___

"Give me that back! That's mine"
    Number of times/week this phrase is said to you by:
    Peer #1: ___   Peer #2 ___   Peer #3 ___   Peer #4 ___

"Stop saying that!"
    Number of times/week this phrase is said to you by:
    Peer #1: ___   Peer #2 ___   Peer #3 ___   Peer #4 ___

Peers can insert their own phrase here: _____
    Number of times/week this phrase is said to you by:
    Peer #1: ___   Peer #2 ___   Peer #3 ___   Peer #4 ___

SCORE YOUR RESULTS: If adults or peers must comment on your aggressiveness more than:
    8 or more times each week: Others have a problem with your aggressive behavior.
    12 or more times: Your aggressiveness is a big problem to others.
    More than 18 times: Everyone but you may be noticing your aggressive conduct.

Lesson 2

Are You the Only One Who Doesn't Think You're Aggressive?

Goal: To assist aggressive students who deny that they have a problem with aggressiveness, to notice that their behavior is considered aggressive by others.

Materials: Chalkboard, chalk, one copy for each student of "Is There an Aggressive Face in the Mirror?" handout, pens.

1. ▲ Inform the students that they will be learning about how to tell if someone really is, or is not aggressive. **Distribute** the "Is There an Aggressive Face in the Mirror?" handout and **ask** the students to each complete the left side of the page by determining which picture of each set best represents their behavior, then marking the proper box in the "I Say" column. **Assist** the class to accurately complete the "Everyone Else Says" portion of the page for each student, one student at a time. **Discuss** with each class member any discrepancy between the student's evaluation, and the class's evaluation, and **note** that the student holds just one opinion, while the class members represent many viewpoints.

2. ▲ Ask the class to interpret and discuss any discrepancies between students' self-appraisals and the peers' appraisals of their aggressiveness. **Assist** the students to consider the following issues during the discussion:
   • Name other times that you have noticed people evaluating their behavior very differently than those around them. *(Stealing, substance abuse, eating disorders, lying, cheating and other times when people do not want to face the truth about their behavior.)*
   • Denial is the term used to describe when a person is the only one (or is one of just a few people) who does not identify a personal problem that is readily identified by others.
   • Denial is part of the problem because until you admit you have a problem, you won't be working on making any changes. Denial can leave you stuck in your problems.
   • If your problems strongly impact others, but you deny there's a problem, there is little chance to work out the problem in a way that is satisfactory to everyone. Solutions are more likely to be mandated, punitive and not within your control.

3. ▲ Ask the students to list other behaviors that may be denied by people. **Include** behaviors such as lying, cheating, irresponsibility, lateness, stealing, substance abuse, eating disorders, etc., and **list** these behaviors in a column on the board. **Ask** the students to determine the likely results of denial for each of these problems, and **list** their responses in a second column on the board. **Include** responses such as "the alcoholic loses his driver's license" and "the kid that cheats, is kicked out of school." **Discuss** the completed list with the class, and **assist** them to determine that denial often does lead to unpleasant consequences for the person with the problem.

4. ▲ Review the major points of this lesson:
   • Denial is the term used to describe when a person is the only one (or is one of just a few people) who does not identify a personal problem that is readily identified by others. If others feel that you are aggressive, but you do not see it or won't admit it, you are probably in denial.
   • Denial is a serious concern because until you admit you have a problem, you can not change the problem.
   • If your problems strongly impact others, but you deny there's a problem, there is little chance to work out the problem in a way that is satisfactory to everyone. Solutions are more likely to be mandated, punitive and not within your control.

Is There an Aggressive Face in the Mirror?

When you look in the mirror, what do you look like? What does everyone else say?

I Say	**Are You Peaceful?**	**Are You Aggressive?**	**Everyone Else Says...**
☐ Aggressive ☐ Peaceful	*Peaceful Look*	*Aggressive Look*	☐ Aggressive ☐ Peaceful
☐ Aggressive ☐ Peaceful	*Peaceful Sound*	*Aggressive Sound*	☐ Aggressive ☐ Peaceful
☐ Aggressive ☐ Peaceful	*Peaceful Interactions*	*Aggressive Interactions*	☐ Aggressive ☐ Peaceful
☐ Aggressive ☐ Peaceful	*Peaceful to Property*	*Aggressive to Property*	☐ Aggressive ☐ Peaceful

Lesson 3

So, What Are You So Mad About Anyway?

Goal: To assist students to better identify the causes of anger and aggression.

Materials: Chalkboard, chalk, one copy for each student of "What Really Causes Anger?" handout, pens, index cards (have enough cards so that each student receives at least five to ten cards.)

1. ▲ Inform the students that they will be learning more about the causes of anger and aggression. **Distribute** the index cards to the students and **ask** them to write (or draw) on each card, one thing that might cause a person to become angry. **Offer** the following items as the type of things they may wish to include: "Dad yells at me", "I miss the bus" and "I have a test in math class." **Collect** the completed cards and **review** them with the class, acknowledging that there are many things that can cause people to become angry. **Retain** the cards for use later in the class.

2. ▲ Ask the students to explain the phrase "the last straw" (or "the straw that broke the camel's back"), and **assist** them to determine that this phrase refers to the event in a chain of anger-provoking occurrences, that evokes rage for that event as well as many or all of the preceding problems. **Note** that the "last straw" is often not a negative or anger-provoking event, but provides an opportunity to express rage for the accumulation of events. **Ask** the students to discuss if they have ever gotten angry at the "wrong" person after having many anger-provoking events happen, and then finally raging at the person who was involved or nearby when the "last straw" happened. **Identify** that the original anger-provoking events can be called "sources of rage", and that when people or events unfairly or disproportionately become the outlets for that rage, they can be called "targets of rage". **Discuss** these concepts with the students.

3. ▲ Distribute the copies of "What Really Causes Anger?" to the class, and ask the students to complete the form as shown in the instructions on that page. **Discuss** the completed forms with the class.

▲ **Ask** the students to sort the index cards into sources and targets of rage, and **note** that there may be more than one way to sort the cards. **Discuss** the results with the students. **Ask** the students to consider if they ever direct their anger at targets rather than sources of rage.

4. ▲ Review the major points of this lesson:
● There are many events that can provoke anger. Sources of rage are events that thoroughly anger you. Targets of rage is a term that can be used to describe when people or events unfairly or disproportionately become the outlets for your rage
● Many people find that they do not direct their anger at the sources of their rage, but at targets.

What Really Causes Anger?

Find the real sources of rage, and also find the targets of rage, that are often mistakenly labeled as sources. Sources of rage are the things that really make you mad through and through. Targets of rage are the things that you may get mad at, but are not really the main source of your anger, but become the target of your anger release. Under each frame of each cartoon strip, write whether the picture shows a source or target of rage.

Lesson 4

The Problem with Scapegoats

Goal: To assist students to better recognize how they may unfairly take out their anger on people and things, and to discover that scapegoating is not an effective way to process and release anger.

Materials: Chalkboard, chalk.

1. ▲ Inform the students that they will be learning about the effectiveness of scapegoating as a way to manage and vent anger. **Discuss** the following brief scenarios with the class, **focusing** on whether scapegoating (taking anger out on another person or thing) solved the problem or added a problem:

• *Brenda's mom really hollered at her before she left to school, then hollered at her again when she returned home. During dinner, Brenda felt her mom just harked at her about her bangs being in her eyes. Right after dinner, Brenda beat up her little sister.*

• *That vice-principal was out to get him. Carlos was sure of that. It infuriated him when the vice-principal would comment on his lateness, and reminded him again to stay out of trouble. Today, the vice-principal had even threatened to give him detention if he was late again. "He doesn't even care that I may have a really good reason to be late. He just threatens me. That really makes me so mad, I might just make prank calls to his house like other kids do."*

• *The older kids just shoved Chris as he moved slowly through the crowded halls. "It was like being stuck in a group of over-sized cattle," he thought to himself as he dodged a student who was in his path. What he hated most was the older kids who poked and pushed him for no good reason. When he got to his locker, he let a swear word slip out: his locker was jammed again. He drew his foot back and kicked it hard into the locker door just as a teacher came around the corner.*

2. ▲ Ask the students to rate the effectiveness of scapegoating people and things to become outlets for anger. **Assist** the students to determine that scapegoating often does not solve problems, but often does create additional problems. **Ask** the students to discuss if they ever scapegoat others, and if this scapegoating is effective or ineffective for them.

3. ▲ Ask the students to identify alternatives to scapegoating for the three vignettes shown above, and **assist** the students to compare the effectiveness of these alternatives with scapegoating. **Include** options such as "talk it out", "ask for help" and "find out how others have handled the situation." **Assist** the students to identify alternatives to scapegoating that they could use in their own lives. **Assist** the students to discuss if scapegoating will work well for them as adults.

4. ▲ Review the major points of this lesson:

• **Scapegoating is the term used to describe taking your anger out on another person or thing.**

• **Scapegoating often does not solve problems. Scapegoating often adds a problem.**

• **There are many effective alternatives to scapegoating others as a way to manage and release your anger.**

• **Scapegoating is often an ineffective anger control device for adults.**

Lesson 5

Could You Have Misdirected Anger?

Goal: To assist students who take out their anger on other people or things, to manage their anger in more appropriate ways.

Materials: Chalkboard, chalk.

1. ▲ **Inform** the students that they will be learning about replacing ineffective anger control methods with more beneficial ways. **Discuss** the following brief scenarios with the class, **focusing** on whether the angry student's rage seems to be out of proportion (too much) for the situation or problem described:

• *Jackson slumped in his chair. "Could you sit up?" Mrs. Rosenberg asked quietly. Jackson shot her an angry look, but said nothing. "Jackson, did you hear me?" she asked with just a trace of annoyance in her voice. It was clear from the way she wrinkled her forehead that she was fairly confused by his silence. "That's it! I'm outta here. You've got it in for me just like the others. I quit!" Jackson shot back as he stormed out the classroom door.*

• *Pop had promised to take a day off to go to the game with Shauna. Here it was Sunday, and he still hadn't called, and there wasn't much time left to get to the stadium. It was just like him. Shauna moped, trying to decide whether to call him at his office. Finally, around 11 AM the phone rang. "Hey Shauna, it's Pedro. Sorry, but I've got to baby sit my brothers Thursday night. No way Mom's gonna let me study with you for that test that night." Shauna cut him off: "Forget it. I don't need your help. I'll just flunk. I shoulda known not to count on ya'. Some boyfriend you are!"*

• *Being the new kid was worse than Lee had imagined. He didn't see any other Asian kids, and it seemed like most of his classmates were a lot taller than him. He was glad the first day at school was over. He felt so left out. No one talked to him, and one girl had made a joke about his accent. Now, his mother was late to pick him up. He felt awkward waiting alone for her car to turn the corner. Everyone else seemed to be in groups. Finally the car pulled in. She had brought their old, battered car, not their newer one. "How could you be so late? I've waited at least ten minutes," Lee demanded as he leaped in the car. Raising his voice louder, he continued before she answered, "And, why did you bring this piece of junk? Now, everyone will think that we don't belong here. Now I'll never fit in. How could you do this to me?!"*

2. ▲ **Define** "misdirected anger" as rage that is out of proportion to the occurrence that prompted the rage. **Ask** the students to consider if they have ever had or witnessed misdirected anger. **Ask** the students to give examples of misdirected anger that they have observed. **List** the students' responses on the board, then **ask** the students to rate the effectiveness of misdirected anger as a problem-solver. **Assist** the students to grade each item on the board, then **determine** if misdirected anger is a good problem-solver.

3. ▲ **Ask** the students to identify the types of problems that are most likely to result in people shifting their anger to other people and things. **Assist** the students to determine that the more important, sensitive and difficult the problem is, the more likely it becomes that that problem will result in shifted anger because acknowledging anger over big problems like a parent's drug abuse or the death of a friend, can be very hard, but blowing up in a familiar way at a familiar target can be easy.

▲ **Ask** each student, one at a time, to respond to the following points, and discuss with the class:
• Which issues are most likely to result in you misdirecting anger?
• Who or what is the familiar target that you often shift anger to?
• What is the familiar way that you shift anger?
• How well does misdirecting anger work to solve problems?
• What other ways could you manage anger that might be more effective than misdirecting it?

4. ▲ Review the major points of this lesson:
• **Misdirected anger is rage that is out of proportion to the event that prompted the rage.**
• **Misdirected anger is an ineffective problem-solver.**
• **The more important, sensitive and difficult the problem is, the more likely it becomes that that problem will result in shifted anger.**
• **There are many effective alternatives to misdirecting anger.**

Lesson 6

Could You Have Lots of Misdirected Anger?

Goal: To further assist students who take out their anger on other people or things, to manage their anger in more appropriate ways.

Materials: Chalkboard, chalk, assorted art and recording supplies (clay, finger paint, wire, string, rope, tape, newspaper, markers, paper, glue, pens, paint, magazines, scissors, audio tape recorder, blank audio tapes, optional video camera and video tapes, etc.)

1. ▲ **Inform** the students that they will be learning more about replacing ineffective anger control methods with more beneficial ways. **Define** the term "misdirected anger" as rage that is out of proportion (too much) for the situation or problem that the person is angry about. **Give** and **request** examples of misdirected anger, such as a student blows up at a teacher the morning after a big fight with his mom. **Assist** the students to determine that people tend to most often have misdirected anger about large, important issues that are difficult to manage.

2. ▲ **Distribute** the art supplies, and **ask** the students to draw, paint or somehow recreate their misdirected anger, and to include the following items in their project: *what their misdirected anger looks like, who or what that anger is really meant for, and who or what is the target that is substituted for the source of the anger.* **Encourage** the students to be creative, allowing them to make three dimensional representations, write poetry, create collages, make audio or video tapes, or scribble.

3. ▲ As appropriate, **discuss** the completed projects with the class, **focusing** on the following points as they apply to your class members:
• Feeling rage is normal if you have large problems you are angry about.
• It is often easy to express anger towards safe targets, but can seem impossible to direct the anger towards the person or thing you are really angry about.
• Common, easy targets for misdirected anger are often the people least likely to hit you, yell back or condemn you. Often, teachers, counselors, friends and family members are favorite targets.
• Rage can play a huge role in determining behavior, especially anger expression, even though you may be largely unaware of this important impact.
• If you are fairly unaware of rage on a regular basis, the rage can take over much of your life, especially your expression of anger.
• You may be carrying a great deal of rage that is weighing you down and causing serious problems with aggressiveness and anger control.
• To gain better control over your life, you may need to more directly express your anger towards the person or thing you are really angry about.
• Misdirected anger can drive your life without you even knowing it.

4. ▲ **Review** the major points of this lesson:
• **Misdirected anger is rage that is too much for the situation or problem that the person is angry about.**
• **Feeling rage is normal, but many people find that it is often easy to express anger towards safe targets, but can seem impossible to direct the anger towards the person or thing you are really angry about.**
• **Common targets for misdirected anger are often the people least likely to hit you, yell back or condemn you.**
• **Rage can play a huge role in determining behavior, particularly anger expression, especially if you are unaware of the rage.**
• **If you are fairly unaware of rage, it can take over much of your life, weigh you down, and cause problems with anger control.**
• **To gain better control over your life, you may need to more directly express your anger towards the person or thing you are really angry about.**
• **Misdirected anger can drive your life without you even knowing it.**

Lesson 7

"Outside Anger" That Comes to School

Goal: To assist students who take out their anger on teachers, other school staff, or peers, to recognize that their anger is "outside anger" misdirected towards school.

Materials: Chalkboard, chalk.

1. ▲ **Inform** the students that they will be learning more about replacing ineffective anger control methods with more beneficial ways. **Define** the term "misdirected anger" as rage that is out of proportion (too much) for the situation or problem that the person is angry about. **Give** and **request** examples of misdirected anger occurring in school, such as a student blows up at a teacher the morning after a big fight with his mom. **Ask** the students to determine the answers to the following queries about misdirected anger that occurs in school:
   - Is the real source of the misdirected anger usually a large, important issue that is difficult to manage, or a small, trivial concern? *(The typical source is usually a serious concern.)*
   - Does the real source of the misdirected anger relate to school? *(Often the real source of the anger is a family problem, peer problem or other event unrelated or barely related to school.)*
   - Who is a likely target of misdirected anger: people who are likely to hit and yell back, or people who are most likely to respond without being abusive? *(People who are likely to respond in non-abusive ways are often frequent targets of anger.)*
   - Are the people who are the real sources of the misdirected anger, often quiet, non-abusive people or more often, people who are powerful, and might hit, yell or impose strict sanctions? *(Often, the real sources of anger are powerful people who are likely to hit, yell or impose serious consequences.)*
   - Who are some common people who might be the real source of misdirected anger? *(Peers and family are common sources of rage, but you may find it difficult or unwise to show your anger towards these people.)*
   - At school, which people are the most common targets of misdirected anger? *(Teachers, counselors, principals, and other students.)*

2. ▲ **Ask** the students to each identify the job or business they hope to one day be involved with, and the **assist** the class to determine if misdirected or "outside" anger will be successful in the adult work place. **Assist** the students to determine that outside anger will be problematic in any job or business.

3. ▲ **Ask** the students to identify the likely impact of outside, misdirected anger on jobs, relationships, hobbies, living sites, friendships, etc., and **aid** them to determine that success in these endeavors will be very difficult if a person has substantial outside anger interfering with their behavior.

▲ **Ask** the students to determine if they may have difficulty managing outside anger in school, and **challenge** them to notice their misdirected anger. Students who say they can control their outside anger, but choose not to do so, can be **asked** to demonstrate their skills by controlling their anger over the next week or month. **Assist** the class to discuss when or how students with misdirected anger in school, will learn the skills to better manage their anger if they do not master these skills while in school. **Aid** the class to determine that students who do not master these skills in school will be unable to magically or suddenly acquire these abilities as adults.

4. ▲ Review the major points of this lesson:
   - **Misdirected anger is rage that is too much for the situation that the person is angry about.**
   - **The real source of the outside anger that comes to school, is often a serious family problem, peer problem or other event unrelated or barely related to school.**
   - **People who are likely to respond in non-abusive ways are often frequent targets of anger. In school, teachers, counselors and other students may be easy targets.**
   - **Misdirected anger in jobs, relationships, hobbies, living sites, and friendships will often lead to serious problems.**
   - **School is the place where people learn to manage outside anger. If you do not learn and practice these skills in school, you are unlikely to have these skills as an adult.**

Lesson 8

Do You Really Want to Go Through Life Without Brakes on Your Anger?

Goal: To assist students who deny that they have problems with out of control anger, to consider the lifelong consequences of being out of control.

Materials: Chalkboard, chalk, one copy for each student of "Do You Really Want to Go Through Life Without Brakes on Your Anger?" and "Can an Adult Even Make It Through the Morning With a Temper Like That?" handout, pens.

1. ▲ **Inform** the students that they will be learning more about the likely consequences of having poor anger control. **Ask** the students to identify reasons why young people may claim that they will not need to learn anger control skills, and **elicit** answers such as "blowing up isn't that big a problem" or "I can get by". **Assist** the students to discuss these excuses and to consider the validity of these explanations.

2. ▲ **Distribute** the pens and the copies of "Do You Really Want to Go Through Life Without Brakes on Your Anger?" handout to the students, and **ask** the class to complete the forms as indicated on the handout. **Discuss** the completed forms with the class, **focusing** on one question at a time. **Ask** the students to consider if the excuses offered earlier as explanations for not needing to learn anger control skills, are supported by the information on the handout. **Assist** the students to determine that without anger control skills, a person will have extreme difficulty in many important areas of life.

3. ▲ **Ask** the students to investigate if people can even make it through the morning of a typical adult day without adequate anger control skills. **Distribute** the "Can an Adult Even Make It Through the Morning With A Temper Like That?," and **ask** the students to consider each item, and determine if anger control is needed in each situation described. **Assist** the students to determine that an adult will have difficulty even making it through the morning of a typical day without anger control skills.

▲ **Ask** the students to determine if they could really survive as adults with poor anger control skills, and **assist** the class to decide that students who believe their excuses, and trust that they won't need anger control skills, may be fooling themselves.

4. ▲ Review the major points of this lesson:
• Without anger control skills, a person will have extreme difficulty in many important areas of life.
• An adult will have difficulty even making it through the morning of a typical day without anger control skills.
• Students who believe that they won't need anger control skills when they are adults, may be very surprised when they actually enter the adult world.

Do You Really Want to Go Through Life Without Brakes on Your Anger?

Choose the most likely result of out-of-control anger in each of the following multiple choice questions.

1. Pedro always uses lots of swear words when he loses his temper. He will find that when he cusses out his apartment manager that...
    a. His apartment manager really won't mind loudly being called swear words.
    b. His apartment managers will patiently wait until Pedro works his way through every nasty swear word he knows in both English and Spanish.
    c. Apartment managers will begin eviction proceedings immediately.

2. Kwan Lee makes a nasty hand gesture at people and calls them very insulting names if she has a problem with the way they are driving on the freeway. She has just moved to a much larger city. She is likely to find that in this huge city, when she makes vicious gestures and comments, the other drivers will...
    a. Give her a friendly wave and bright smile.
    b. Ram her car with their's.
    c. Thank her for sharing her feelings so freely.

3. Brad grabs people by the collar when he gets angry at them. Now, Brad has a job he really likes. The first time he grabs a business customer by the collar, he will...
    a. Get a "free trip" from his boss to the unemployment office.
    b. Get a really big raise from his boss.
    c. Get a really big promotion from his boss.

4. Maria sometimes shakes people really hard by the shoulders when she is furious with them. Maria now has two tiny children of her own. When she shakes her children, she will find...
    a. How easy it is to cause a serious injury to a baby.
    b. That her children won't mind being hurt by their mother.
    c. That her children won't mind being scared of their mother.

5. Vanessa spits at people who make her angry. She has her own business now, and the first time she spits at the person who supplies her merchandise, she will discover...
    a. Most business people consider being spit at to be the best part of their job.
    b. Spitting at business acquaintances is a popular business practice like shaking hands.
    c. How quickly business people file big law suits claiming assault.

6. Jack can't keep his hands off of the women he works with. In the work place, this will result in...
    a. A huge sexual harassment law suit against him that he will lose.
    b. A lot of happy co-workers who like to be touched by anybody who has the urge to do so.
    c. Thank-you's from co-workers who like to have their personal space violated at work.

7. Rosemary carries a weapon whether it's allowed or not. When the state trooper pulls her over for a traffic check, he will...
    a. Understand that the rules don't really apply to Rosemary.
    b. Say that she can pick and choose which laws she follows.
    c. Confiscate the weapon and arrest her.

8. At work, Jason makes slurs about women and people of diverse backgrounds. Jason will learn...
    a. That it's good business to harass customers and co-workers.
    b. That sexual and racial harassment will lead to many serious legal consequences.
    c. Slurring others is the best way to win their business and respect.

Can an Adult Even Make It Through the Morning With a Temper Like That?

Roberto has poor anger control skills. Follow Roberto through the morning of one typical day in the life of an adult and determine if adults must have anger control skills to succeed and survive.

Time	Event	Was Anger Control Needed?
3:42 AM	Roberto's son wakes him up for the fourth time that night to again complain that he can't sleep.	☐ Yes ☐ No
4:06 AM	Roberto had just fallen back to sleep when the newspaper boy tosses the newspaper into Roberto's metal porch screen door, waking him up.	☐ Yes ☐ No
4:46 AM	Roberto had once again just fallen back to sleep when his son again wakes him, this time to complain that his pillow wasn't very comfortable.	☐ Yes ☐ No
5:04 AM	Roberto was dozing when the sanitation truck came loudly around the corner, and stopped in front of his house to pick up the trash. The sanitation workers crash and slam the metal trash cans waking Roberto's son up.	☐ Yes ☐ No
5:23 AM	Roberto is woken by his alarm clock going off, but he realizes it went off an hour early. He realizes that he set the clock wrong again.	☐ Yes ☐ No
6:23 AM	Roberto has to wait for his son to finish in the bathroom. He sits shivering on the floor near the bathroom.	☐ Yes ☐ No
7:00 AM	Roberto starts to make breakfast for himself and his son. He realizes that his son has finished all the milk and bread. He can't find anything for breakfast.	☐ Yes ☐ No
7:25 AM	Roberto can not find his bus pass anywhere, and he has no change. He won't be able to take the bus unless he finds some change or the bus pass.	☐ Yes ☐ No
7:34 AM	Roberto's boss calls and yells at him to hurry up, that the whole crew is stuck waiting for him. The boss slams the phone down in Roberto's ear.	☐ Yes ☐ No
7:43 AM	Roberto finds the bus pass in his son's room. Apparently, his son took it out of Roberto's wallet without asking.	☐ Yes ☐ No
7:59 AM	The boss hands Roberto a written warning about his lateness and threatens to fire him if it happens again. He tells Roberto that he's a "crummy employee" and that he regrets hiring him.	☐ Yes ☐ No
8:49 AM	Roberto realizes he has no money for a morning coffee, or lunch, that somehow he has left his wallet at home.	☐ Yes ☐ No

Lesson 9

The Real-World Consequences of Aggression

Goal: To convincingly demonstrate to aggressive students the many consequences that aggressiveness can elicit, and to break through their denial about being aggressive.

Materials: Chalkboard, chalk, newspapers and news magazines (that have stories illustrating the real-world consequences of aggressive acts such as murder, child abuse, harassment, etc.), paper and pens.

1. ▲ **Inform** the students that they will be learning more about the likely consequences of aggressiveness. **Ask** the students to identify the reactions aggressive youth may have to requests to moderate their aggressiveness, and **elicit** answers such as "they deny that they're aggressive" or "they say that it's not a problem." **Assist** the students to discuss who else offers excuses, and denies or minimizes problem behavior. **Elicit** answers such as the following: *alcoholics, drug addicts, people with eating disorders, and people who steal.* **Assist** the students to determine that denying, minimizing or excusing a problem keeps that person from accurately viewing or clearly understanding it.

2. ▲ **Inform** the students that they will be investigating the actual consequences of aggressiveness, and **note** that these consequences will occur whether or not the person acknowledges that there is a problem. **Distribute** the newspapers and news magazines, along with the pens and paper, and **ask** the students to research the likely consequences faced by people with serious anger control problems. **Direct** the students to conduct this research by identifying the consequences of anger control problems such as domestic violence, assault, threats, murder, harassment, verbal abuse, fights, gang conflict, child abuse, spouse abuse, etc. **Discuss** the student's findings with the class, **assisting** the class to determine that serious anger control problems often yield serious consequences such as incarceration, fines, divorce, loss of children, death, loss of job, injury, etc. **Ask** the students to determine if these are consequences they wish to face.

3. ▲ **Ask** the students to consider the effectiveness of denial by investigating whether denying any of the following problems can spare the person from the likely consequences of that problem: *alcoholism, drug abuse, eating disorders, stealing, lying.* **Ask** the students to determine if denying aggressiveness will somehow spare a person from the consequences normally incurred. **Aid** the class to recognize that denial will not spare aggressive people from the real world consequences of their actions.

4. ▲ Review the major points of this lesson:
- Denying, minimizing or excusing a problem such as aggressiveness, keeps that person from accurately viewing or clearly understanding it.
- Serious anger control problems often yield serious consequences such as incarceration, fines, divorce, loss of children, death, loss of job, injury, etc. These are serious consequences most people prefer not to face.
- Denial will not spare an aggressive people from the real world consequences of their actions.

Lesson 10

Could You Have a Problem with Aggression?

Note: This lesson provocatively confronts aggressive students' denial of their anger control problems. This lesson should be used carefully by non-clinicians, such as teachers, who may wish to consult with a mental health professional to best ensure an appropriate, careful and safe implementation of this lesson.

Goal: To break through the denial shown by aggressive students who minimize, excuse or deny that they have critical problems with anger control.

Materials: Chalkboard, chalk, one copy for each student of "The Top 6 Ways to Deny You Have a Problem with Aggression" handout, pens, large sheets of light-colored or white construction paper.

1. ▲ **Inform** the students that they will be learning more about the denial that some aggressive people may have about their problem with aggressiveness. **Ask** the students to identify the reactions aggressive youth often have when confronted about their aggressive behavior, and **elicit** answers such as "they deny that they're aggressive" or "they say that it's not a problem."

▲ **Distribute** the copies of "The Top 6 Ways to Deny You Have a Problem with Aggression" handout, and **discuss** with the class. **Assist** the class members to give feedback to aggressive students who actually use these or similar excuses.

2. ▲ **Assist** the students to relay their concerns to class members who continue to deny, minimize or excuse their aggressive behavior. **Ask** the students to divide into small groups and to make lifelines for and with class members who are still denying their aggressiveness. **Inform** the students that a lifeline is a horizontal line they draw on paper, that lists the major events in a person's life, and the dates the events occurred. **Ask** the students to create two lifelines for each aggressive class member: the first lifeline of hypothetical events should be crafted as though the student learned to manage their aggressiveness; the second lifeline of hypothetical events should be crafted as though the student continued to deny their aggressive behavior and began to experience the expectable, serious consequences of the behavior.

3. ▲ **Discuss** the completed lifelines with the class, **assisting** the students to continue to confront peers who are denying, minimizing or excusing their anger control problems. **Assist** the students to recognize that denial of anger control problems often may lead to extreme consequences such as death, and **aid** them to convey their concern about these outcomes to their peers. **Assist** the students to confront denial, minimizing and excuses, referring to the "Top 6 Ways to Deny You Have a Problem with Aggression" handout, as needed.

▲ **Ask** the students who continue to deny their anger control problems to consent to tracking the number of aggressive incidents that occur in just your school or agency setting. An adult or peer who has extensive contact with the aggressive student, can be asked to keep a tally of all the verbal, physical and property problems that the aggressive youth is involved in during one day or week, then can report the results back to the class to help provide clarification on whether a problem exists or not.

4. ▲ Review the major points of this lesson:
• **Students often use excuses to deny, minimize or explain away their aggressiveness.**
• **Denying a serious anger control problem can often result in extreme consequences, including death.**
• **If those around you see problems with aggressiveness, but you do not, you are probably in denial.**

The Top 6 Ways To
Deny You Have a Problem with Aggression

❻ Force them to see it your way.

❺ Pretend you really like negative consequences... a lot...really...REALLY!

❹ Shut your eyes.

❸ Shut their eyes.

❷ Point the finger elsewhere.

❶ Convince them you'll be able to control your temper when you're an adult.

Lesson 11

Are You the Only One Who Can't See the Warning Label on Your Fist?

Goal: To break through the denial shown by aggressive students who minimize, excuse or deny that they have critical problems with anger control.

Materials: Chalkboard, chalk, art supplies (poster board, construction paper, pens, markers, glue, newspapers, magazines, scissors, tape, etc.), optional recording and playback equipment (audio or video taping and playback equipment, tapes.)

1. ▲ **Inform** the students that they will be learning more about the denial that some aggressive people may have about their problem with aggressiveness. **Ask** the students to identify the reactions aggressive youth often have when confronted about their aggressive behavior, and **elicit** answers such as "they deny that they're aggressive" or "they say that it's not a problem."

▲ **Ask** the students to share stories about, and reactions to people who have denied problems even though "everyone" around them could clearly see the problems that were being denied. **Assist** the class members to discuss denial by alcoholics, people who cheat, people who lie, drug users, people who are physically ill, people who are over-tired, and others. **Assist** the class to discuss the similar concerns and frustrations they feel when someone denies their anger control problems.

2. ▲ **Ask** the students to relay their concerns to class members who continue to deny, minimize or excuse their aggressive behavior; **discuss** these concerns.

▲ **Ask** the students to individually, or in small groups, make educational advertisements about the hazards of denying, minimizing or excusing aggressiveness. **Distribute** the art and recording supplies. **Ask** the students to build their advertisements on the theme of "Are You The Only One Who Can't See the Warning Label on Your Fist?", and to include a focus on the likely consequences of denied anger control problems.

3. ▲ **Discuss** and **review** the completed advertisements with the class, and **assist** the students to develop a plan to post, circulate or publicize their efforts throughout your setting and/or community.

4. ▲ Review the major points of this lesson:
• Even though people may deny their anger control problems, those who are around them, can still clearly see the problem.
• The people who are around the person who denies an anger control problem, often have many concerns and strong feelings about that person and their problem.
• When you can't or won't acknowledge your problems with aggressiveness, it's as though you are the only one who can't read the warning label on your fist.

Lesson 12

Find Work Where Aggression Works

Goal: To assist aggressive students to discover that they may have great difficulty supporting themselves financially via a job, business, or other method, if they lack adequate anger control skills.

Materials: Chalkboard, chalk, one copy for each student of "Can You Really Make a Living With a Temper Like That?" handout.

1. ▲ **Inform** the students that they will be learning more about the consequences of anger control problems in the adult work world. **Ask** the students to speculate on how they expect to financially support themselves as adults. **Elicit** answers such as "own a trucking company" or "work at a factory," and **list** these responses on the board. **Retain** this list for use later in the lesson.

▲ **Ask** the class members to identify the requirements for anger control in the work environments shown on the board, and **list** the students' responses on the board. **Assist** the class to compare the work place requirements for anger control to the requirements of your setting, **aiding** the students to note the many similarities. **Discuss** what is likely to happen to students who are unable to meet these requirements in your setting, when they enter the adult work world. **Examine** the likelihood that students will suddenly or instantly be able to learn and use anger control skills as adults if they have not done so previously. **Assist** the class to determine that students who are currently unable to manage their anger properly will likely become adults with anger control problems in the work place.

2. ▲ **Ask** the students to re-examine their list of potential job and business endeavors. **Ask** the students to cross out any job or business listed on the board that people cannot successfully do if they have serious anger control problems. **Discuss** the completed list, **noting** that few/no job or business opportunities remain, then **ask** how people with anger control problems are going to be able to survive financially if they can't succeed as either an employee or business owner. **Allow** the students to suggest excuses and explanations of how they will be able to survive financially despite their anger problems.

3. ▲ **Inform** the students that they will be investigating if it is possible that there are valid excuses and explanations of how people with anger problems can earn a living despite their aggressiveness. **Distribute** the "Can You Really Make a Living With a Temper Like That?" handout, and **review** the form with the class, examining one frame at a time. **Assist** the students to determine that the excuses and explanations appear invalid, and that anger control problems are very likely to create major problems in the work arena, and can impede their ability to become and remain financially self-supporting. **Ask** the students to list all the jobs and businesses that a person with extreme anger control problems can succeed in, then **note** that there are few/no options.

4. ▲ Review the major points of this lesson:
● If you have not learned and used anger control skills as a youth, you are unlikely to suddenly or instantly be able to acquire and use anger control skills as an adult.
● Few/no job or business opportunities exist for adults with serious anger control problems.
● People with serious anger control problems often have great difficulty maintaining a job or business, and consequently often have major problems with financial survival.
● If you believe that you will be able to evade the consequences of your aggressiveness in the work place by relying on welfare, a gang, illegal activity or a wealthy spouse, you are likely to discover that your anger control problems will produce similar problems and similar negative results in these areas. One way or the other, your aggressiveness is likely to make it hard for you to survive financially, regardless of any excuses or explanations.

Can You REALLY Make a Living With a Temper Like That?

To be successfully involved in most jobs and businesses, people need anger management skills. Some people who lack anger management skills, believe that they will be able to support themselves even though they can't control their tempers. Here are some of the reasons they believe that they will be able to survive financially as adults. Do you believe these explanations and excuses?

"Swear at me! That's what I pay you for—...NOT"

"My boss won't care that much if I blow up once in a while."

"You're outta here! We're TIRED of the yelling!!"

"My family will always take care of me-- no matter what!"

WELFARE
—NOTICE—
Welfare is now WORKFARE. You must work to get ANY HELP!

"I'll just go on welfare."

"My gang will take care of me."

"We want to hire you but first want to talk to your LAST BOSS!"

"I'll just get another job."

DIVORCE DECREE
Marriage ended due to CRUEL TREATMENT

"I'll marry a wealthy person."

"Man, I don't need this fighting. I'm CUTTING YOU OFF!"

"I can just deal drugs."

"I'll just start my own business so I can do what I want."

Lesson 13

Do You Control Your Anger, or Does It Control You?

Goal: To teach students to acknowledge responsibility for their aggressiveness.

Materials: Chalkboard, chalk, one copy for each student of "Who Really Controls Your Fist, Mouth and Actions?" handout, paper, pens.

1. ▲ **Inform** the students that they will be learning about moderating aggressiveness. **Ask** the class members to identify the excuses that students sometimes offer to deflect responsibility when confronted with having used aggressive behaviors such as hitting, kicking, talking back to an adult, swearing or causing property damage. **Elicit** answers such as "he made me hit him" or "I didn't mean to do it."

▲ **Ask** the class to investigate the validity of these excuses. **Distribute** the copies of "Who Really Controls Your Fist, Mouth and Actions?" to the students, and **review** and **discuss** with the class. **Assist** the class to debunk each of the excuses pictured on the handout, and to determine that each person is in charge of their behavior.

2. ▲ **Distribute** the pens and paper, and **ask** the students to draw cartoons similar to those shown in the handout, that debunk other popular excuses that are commonly offered to deflect responsibility for aggression. **Discuss** the completed cartoons with the class.

3. ▲ **Discuss** the following points with the class:
   • You cannot take responsibility for your aggressiveness until you acknowledge that you are the boss of your actions.
   • If you are not in charge of your aggressiveness, who is? Who else operates your mouth muscles, fist and feet? *(No one else.)*
   • Excuses that deflect responsibility from you are not true. You are the only one who can operate your mouth, fist and feet.
   • How can class members work to help each other when excuses are offered for aggressiveness? *(By confronting the excuses as inaccurate every time an excuse is offered.)*
   • How well will excuses for aggressiveness work in the adult world? *(They won't work.)*
   • What can you say when you hear an excuse for aggressiveness? *(You can use phrases such as "Yes, you may not have meant to do that, but you are still responsible for doing it.")*

4. ▲ Review the major points of this lesson:
   • Sometimes people offer excuses for their aggressiveness that deflect the responsibility for the actions away from them.
   • Each person is in charge of their own behavior, not anyone or anything else.
   • You cannot take responsibility for your aggressiveness until you acknowledge that you are the boss of your actions.
   • Excuses that deflect responsibility are not true. Only you can operate your mouth, hands and feet. No one or nothing else can.
   • Excuses for aggression will not work in the adult world.
   • When you hear an excuse for aggression, confront it, don't accept it.

Who REALLY Controls Your Fist, Mouth and Actions?

Students often offer excuses for their aggressive behavior. Review the following cartoons to determine if these excuses are accurate. Do you think that students have the ability to control their own behavior, or can other people or things operate their fist, mouth and actions for them?

"Hey, JERK"

"Yes, YOU, BUFFALO FACE"

"I HAD to hit him!"

"Hey, YOU! Hey, Pea brain"

"PINHEAD!"

"Hairless WONDER"

Principal

"I DIDN'T MEAN to DO IT"

POKE

POKE

POKE POKE POKE POKE POKE

POW

"He MADE ME DO IT"

EXAM

EXA

EXAM

EXAM CHEATING

"I TRIED TO STOP IT!"

"I HAD NO CHOICE BUT TO TAKE IT"

Lesson 14

Spot Aggression Before It (Or You) Strikes

Goal: To teach students to anticipate and control their aggressive behavior.

Materials: Chalkboard, chalk, one copy for each student of "Can You Spot Aggression Before It (Or You) Strikes?" handout, a stop watch.

1. ▲ Inform the students that they will be learning about moderating aggressiveness. **Ask** the class members to identify and discuss the pace at which aggressive incidents seem to unfold. **Assist** the class to focus on how rapidly these events can seem to unfold, and how they are often surprised by the events that occur and the consequences that follow. **Ask** the students to identify the excuses that students sometimes offer that blame the speed at which the event took place. **Elicit** answers such as "I didn't have time to think first" and "It happened too fast to think about it."

▲ Ask the class to investigate the validity of these excuses. **Distribute** the copies of "Can You Spot Aggression Before It (Or You) Strikes?" handout, and **review** and **discuss** with the class. **Assist** the class to debunk each of the excuses pictured on the handout, and to determine that there are many opportunities for students to consider their actions. **Ask** the students to identify the times that the cartoon characters in each of the strips, could have paused and thought. **Assist** them to determine that in the cartoons, as in real life, there are many opportunities for thinking prior to, and during an aggressive episode.

2. ▲ Tell the following joke to the students: *What are the only two places that aggressive kids can think? Answer: In the back of a police car, and in the principal's office.* **Discuss** the joke with the class members **assisting** them to determine that students will be thinking about their aggressive misbehavior one way or the other, but that thinking after the event can not change what has happened, but thinking prior to the event can prevent misbehavior.

▲ Discuss with the students that their involvement in aggression can seem to occur at a speed that appears similar to the way a TV looks when they fast-forward through a videotape. **Assist** the students to discuss how they could slow that speed to become more like the way the TV looks when they slowly click frame by frame through a videotape.

3. ▲ Assist the students to identify incidents when they have become, or are likely to become aggressive, then **aid** them to develop times they could think prior to the event occurring. **Assist** the students to each develop a phrase that they could think about to help them avoid aggression. **Ensure** that the phrases are positively worded, for example, **use** the phrase "hands to self" rather than "don't hit." **Challenge** the students to become the fastest in the class at saying their phrase. **Use** a stop watch to time the number of repetitions each class member can say in 10 seconds. **Discuss** with the students how they can remember, and really use these phrases to think prior to getting involved in, or during aggressive activities.

4. ▲ Review the major points of this lesson:
• **Sometimes people offer excuses for their aggressiveness that claim there was "no time" to think first.**
• **There are many opportunities for thinking prior to, and during an aggressive episode.**
• **It is possible to slow the speed at which aggressive behavior seems to occur.**
• **There is always time to think before or during an aggressive incident. When called on, be ready to say the phrase you will tell yourself to remind yourself to select peaceful conduct. Also, be ready to tell when you will use this phrase.**

Can You Spot Aggressiveness Before It (Or You) Strikes?

Students often say that there was not enough time to think before or during the time they are aggressive. Is that really true? Look at the cartoons below and the explanations offered for aggressiveness, then decide if there is time to think about aggressiveness before it-- or you-- strikes.

Lesson 15

There Must Be 10,000 Ways to Keep Your Temper

Goal: To teach students to use new anger control methods.

Materials: Chalkboard, chalk.

1. ▲ Inform the students that they will be learning more about anger control. **Ask** the class members to discuss whether it is easy or hard to control their tempers, and whether there appear to be many good methods of anger control. **Assist** the class to determine that for many students, anger control can be quite challenging, and that there can appear to be few good anger control methods.

2. ▲ Acknowledge to the students that developing good anger control can be challenging, but that there may be more anger control methods than they realize. **Ask** the students to identify the "10,000 Ways to Keep Your Temper", and **write** their responses on the board. **Include** the following anger control strategies: *stop and think first, walk away, think about the consequences, draw your anger on paper, write out your anger, hit a punching bag, scream into a pillow, go to a counselor, tell a friend, distract yourself, read a book or magazine, talk a walk, take a run, take a hot bath, take a shower, tear up some paper, find something to do, call a friend, talk to the person who provoked your anger, visualize your dreams and hopes, breathe deeply and slowly, run up a flight of stairs, write an angry letter, find an adult to talk to, talk yourself into staying peaceful, tell yourself that this will pass, learn to let go, remember your goals, think about what will best help you in the long run, think again before taking action, wait 24 hours before taking action, imagine the other person's point of view, turn it over to a higher power, get a back rub, put it aside until tomorrow.*

3. ▲ Ask the students to each select five anger control methods they could use, and then **discuss** how they could use these methods in their actual most challenging situations. **Assist** the students to role-play using these methods in simulations of their actual situations, then **debrief** the role-plays with the class.

4. ▲ Review the major points of this lesson:
• **For many students, anger control can be quite challenging, and there can appear to be few good anger control methods.**
• **While developing good anger control can be challenging for some students, there are many anger control methods that you can use to improve your control.**
• **By using improved anger control methods, you can successfully manage your temper more often.**

Lesson 16

How to Keep a Grip on Yourself

Goal: To teach students about the different types of anger, and to use new anger control methods.

Materials: Chalkboard, chalk.

1. ▲ Inform the students that they will be learning more about anger control. **Ask** the class members to discuss the difficulties they have effectively regulating their anger. **Inform** the class that in this lesson, they will learn more about the different types of anger they face.

▲ Discuss with the students that there are four types of anger, and **review** this information as shown below, **writing** on the board, the key points to remember:
• *Immediate anger: this is anger that is right in front of you, such as another student just punched you.*
• *Brewing anger: this is anger that starts out small and becomes bigger and stronger, such as you hear from a friend that another student wants to hit you, and the more that you think about that, the madder you get.*
• *Accumulated anger: this is anger that you've been carrying a long time, even though the actual anger-provoking event may have stopped. For example, you were hit nearly every day several years ago by the neighborhood bully, but you are still pretty mad about it even though he stopped hitting you years ago.*
• *Leftover anger: this is anger that could have been vented and put in the past, but instead you continue to be angry and there is no end to the episode. For example: a kid hits you once and apologizes, but you never stop being mad about it no matter how he attempts to make amends to you.*

2. ▲ Inform the students that they may want to deal with each type of anger differently. **Review** these differences, as shown below, **adding** to the board the key points you want your students to remember:
• *Immediate anger: Your job is to control yourself while resolving the problem. Best methods: talk it out, leave the area until you cool off, compromise.*
• *Brewing anger: Your job is to notice that you are growing madder so you can control it. Best methods: solve the problem, talk out your anger, keep a watch over your anger level, be prepared for unplanned outbursts.*
• *Accumulated anger: Your job is to stay aware of how angry you are, and to control yourself. If possible, your work is to express or resolve your anger. Best methods: express your anger to the person, ask the person to make restitution or amends, and keep a watch over your anger level because you are at risk of unplanned outbursts.*
• *Leftover anger: Your job is to work to end the episode and put your anger to rest. Best methods: figure out why you haven't put your anger to rest yet, keep a watch for unplanned outbursts, get the anger out, and end the episode.*

▲ Ask the students to suggest other good methods to cope with each of the four types of anger.

3. ▲ Ask the students to each determine what types of anger they most often have, and **assist** them to select the methods that they could use to better control their anger. **Assist** the students to compare and contrast the results of using these anger control methods vs. not using them. **Ask** the students to determine which results they prefer.

4. ▲ Review the major points of this lesson:
• **There are four types of anger. Immediate anger is when you are angry about an event that just happened.**
• **Brewing anger is anger that starts out small and becomes bigger and stronger over time as you think about it.**
• **Accumulated anger is anger that you've been carrying a long time, even though the actual anger-provoking event may have stopped.**
• **Leftover anger is anger that could have been vented and put in the past, but instead you continue to be angry, and there is no end to the episode.**
• **You may need to use different approaches to successfully control the different types of anger you face.**

Lesson 17

The Truth About Anger

Goal: To teach students that anger is an expectable, normal occurrence, and to provide additional information on anger management.

Materials: Chalkboard, chalk, art supplies (such as paper, paint, pens, glue, string, magazines, newspapers, scissors, paint brushes, markers, pens, poster board, construction paper, etc.)

1. ▲ **Inform** the students that they will be learning more about anger control. **Ask** the class members if they have ever heard statements like the following: "don't get mad", "hold it in and take it like a man", "you have a bad temper", "be a good girl and don't get mad" and "you have no right to be mad about this." **Assist** the students to identify additional phrases that people sometimes use to squash, delay or downplay anger. **Assist** the class to recognize that anger is quite frequently squashed, minimized, delayed or referred to negatively. **Note** that it is easy to come to believe that it is bad or wrong to feel anger, but in reality, anger is a normal, healthy occurrence.

2. ▲ **Ask** the students to speculate on how children learn to identify and manage anger, and **assist** the class to determine that children learn anger management and identification by watching their family. **Assist** the students to discuss how family members may identify and manage anger, and **include** answers such as "they drink beer if they get mad" and "my sister just grinds her teeth and says she's not mad when she's still furious." **Inform** the students that children who grow up in homes where anger is medicated with drugs, food or alcohol; denied; forbidden; or acted out violently, often do not have the chance to learn positive ways to identify and manage anger.

3. ▲ **Inform** the students that they will be learning more about identifying anger. **Distribute** the art supplies and **ask** the students to draw anger. Students may make abstract reproductions, create pictures of angry people, or similar projects. **Discuss** the completed projects with the class, and include the following facts about anger in the discussion:

- *You can not turn on or off anger anymore than you can simply decide to stop feeling pain when injured. If you feel anger, you feel it.*
- *While there is "nothing wrong" with anger, there is a lot wrong with expressing anger in ways that hurt yourself, others or property. Sometimes people see only the problems with your expression of anger, and forget that the feeling is fine, just the way you express it, is not so fine.*
- *You can pretend you are not mad, but the anger usually doesn't go away. Often, it will sneak out in problem ways. Problems with drugs, eating disorders and violence often relate to anger.*
- *If you look at how your family manages anger, you can get an idea of the approaches you may either heavily use or avoid.*
- *You are not "good" or "bad" based on how you deal with your anger. A better way to think about anger is to determine if you use healthy or problematic ways of managing it.*
- *Like quitting smoking or losing weight, changing a problem with anger is often a slow, not instantaneous process that will likely include some successes and failures.*
- *When learning anger control, expect to gradually improve, and to make occasional mistakes although the trend of change should be towards improvement if you are successfully changing.*

4. ▲ Review the major points of this lesson:
- **Because people often make negative comments about anger, it is easy to believe that it is bad or wrong to feel anger. In reality, anger is a normal, healthy occurrence.**
- **Children who grow up in homes where anger is medicated with drugs, food or alcohol; denied; forbidden; or acted out violently, often do not have the chance to learn positive ways to identify and manage anger.**
- **There is much misinformation and ignorance about the real facts about anger. Here are some true facts: If you feel anger, you can't simply stop feeling it. There is "nothing wrong" with anger, just in the problematic ways it is expressed. Anger usually doesn't go away if you deny it, and repressed anger often leads to other problems. Making changes in how you manage anger is usually a gradual, up-and-down process.**

Lesson 18

Who Does Aggression Really Hurt?

Goal: To assist students to recognize that their aggressiveness hurts them more than anybody or anything else.

Materials: Chalkboard, chalk, pens, paper.

1. ▲ **Inform** the students that they will be learning more about the consequences of aggression. **Ask** the class members to speculate on how much time aggressive students use up when they become involved in problematic aggressive conduct and the consequences of this behavior. **Assist** the students to theorize that a substantial number of hours each day is spent on aggressive conduct. **Assist** the students to consider how else this theoretical number of hours could be used, and **assist** them to offer responses such as "earning money", "becoming a good rapper" or "skateboarding." **Assist** the class to discuss what kind of lasting results are gained by investing time in problems with aggressiveness. **Ask** the aggressive students to consider if they have "better things to do with their time."

2. ▲ **Distribute** the pens and paper. **Ask** the students to write two letters to the instructor. **Inform** the students that both letters should be dated 20 years from today and should specifically describe what has happened to the student during that time period. **Inform** the students that the first letter should be written as though the student gained anger control skills, and the letter should reflect the results the student obtained now that the aggressiveness is in control. **Ask** the students to write the second letter as if the student did not acquire anger control skills, and the events described should reflect this lack of control. As needed, **have** the students work in pairs or small groups with the class members assisting each other to honestly complete this task. If there are students who resist completing the task honestly, assign one or more peers to complete the task for them.

▲ **Review** and **discuss** the letters, considering one student's set of letters at a time.

3. ▲ **Ask** the students to discuss what they really want to do with the rest of their lives-- waste it on aggressiveness or live their dreams.

4. ▲ **Review the major points of this lesson:**
 • If you have problems with anger control, you may find that you must devote a substantial number of hours each day to dealing with that aggressive conduct. There may be uses of that time that would be a lot more fun, pleasant and productive.
 • If you learn to manage your aggressiveness, you may be able to live your life in a way that you find rewarding, pleasant and fulfilling.
 • If you do not learn to manage your aggressiveness, you may live your life coping with your anger control problems and the consequences of your lack of control.
 • We all get just one life. Most of us do not want to waste our only chance on aggressiveness. Most people would rather live their dreams, not waste them.

Lesson 19

Turn Down the Heat at Home

Goal: To assist students to better control their anger at home.

Materials: Chalkboard, chalk.

1. ▲ **Inform** the students that they will be learning about managing their anger at home. **Ask** the class to discuss whether it is easier or harder to manage their temper at home vs. elsewhere. **Assist** the students to determine that many people find it harder to avoid tantrums, verbal abuse, and other aggressiveness at home. **Assist** the students to consider why it can seem harder to manage anger at home, and **elicit** responses such as "there's lots of old problems" and "we've got lots of fights that happen over and over again."

2. ▲ **Ask** the students to identify the typical situations at home that result in problems with anger control. **Assist** the class to aid each student to develop a plan to maintain control despite how other family members may behave. **Include** strategies such as the following: *walk away; anticipate problems and avoid them; remember that if others act aggressively, you don't have to; stop and think first; remember how horrible you will feel afterwards if you lose control; distract yourself; look for a compromise; plan to never name call; plan to never scream; use a business-like manner no matter what others do; watch for and avoid the pattern that family problems sometimes take; refuse to argue; get help from a counselor, religious leader or other adult; avoid the places and subjects that fights often involve; comply with reasonable parental instructions; say "yes" to parents instead of constant "no"; think about what else your family could accomplish if they weren't arguing so much of the time.* **Ask** the students to role-play using these methods, then **debrief** each role-play, and **redo** as necessary.

3. ▲ **Ask** the students to discuss how they feel when they become enmeshed in chronic family fights. **Assist** the students to identify the strong, lasting negative feelings and other significant consequences that they encounter, then **ask** them to determine which option they prefer: *to refuse to become enmeshed in family fights and avoid many of the negative feelings and consequences OR become enmeshed and have to cope with serious consequences and many lasting, residual feelings.*

▲ To best illustrate the futility of family fights, **ask** one of the students who is most resistive to using better anger control at home, to pick up a book that you've placed on the floor. After the student picks up the book, **toss** it back on the floor, then **ask** the student to pick it up again, then you **toss** it down again. **Repeat** several times, then **discuss** with the class that this "wasted effort" is what family life can be like unless one or more of the family members, such as you, opt to not initiate, join in or further family fights.

4. ▲ Review the major points of this lesson:
  • It can seem harder to manage anger at home than anywhere else.
  • There are many strategies that you can use to avoid anger control problems and family fights at home.
  • Often, when you lose control of your anger at home, afterward, you may feel lasting, serious negative feelings, and have to face unpleasant consequences. By opting to work to refrain from anger control problems at home, you can reduce the amount of consequences and unpleasant feelings you must cope with.
  • Repetitive family fights sometimes make as much sense as picking up and dropping a book over and over: nothing of value is accomplished. You may wish to be one of the family members who chooses to control their anger at home.

Lesson 20

Make This Tantrum Your Last

Goal: To assist students to learn new ways of managing their anger.

Materials: Chalkboard, chalk, one copy for each student of "Taming Your Temper: An Owner's Manual" handout.

1. ▲ Inform the students that they will be learning about making lasting changes in their anger control strategies. **Distribute** the copies of "Taming Your Temper: An Owner's Manual," and **discuss** it, **reviewing** one step at a time in detail.

2. ▲ Ask the students to identify how they could use the steps to anger control that are pictured in the handout, in the typical situations they encounter that result in anger control problems. **Assist** the class to aid each student to develop a specific plan to use these steps to manage likely future problem situations. Possible uses of the steps include the following: *posting the manual on a locker door, desk top or door; memorizing the steps; planning to use the steps that are most often forgotten; keeping the manual close by in a back pack or wallet; making large posters of the steps and posting them prominently in many places; posting the steps in locations where problems have occurred, or could occur; and planning to systematically use the steps every time an anger-provoking situation emerges or appears imminent.*

3. ▲ Ask the students to discuss where else or when else they will have the opportunity to learn anger control. **Assist** the students to determine that there are usually few other opportunities to learn anger management, and that these opportunities usually diminish as you get older while the consequences for aggressiveness become more serious. **Aid** the class to notice that this help is one of the few chances they may have to receive non-punitive assistance with their anger. **Assist** the class to notice that if students do not work to make consistent improvements to their serious anger control problems, they run the risk that future responses to their aggressiveness could take a much more punitive form, such as jail time, law suits, divorce, child abuse charges, getting fired, etc.

4. ▲ Review the major points of this lesson:

• **You can systematically learn to control your anger. The first step is to predict the future and anticipate problems.**

• **The second step to controlling your anger is to stop and think before taking any action.**

• **The third step to controlling your anger is to find all the choices you have to select from.**

• **The fourth step to controlling your anger is to evaluate and rate the choices.**

• **The fifth step to controlling your anger is to select the best choice.**

• **The sixth step to controlling your anger is to stick with your decision.**

• **Adults with serious anger control problems often are give punishments or sanctions such as being fired, being sued, losing their kids, or going to jail. Using the help that you are receiving now to control your anger, is one of the few times you may be offered non-punitive help. If you choose not to use this help and opt continue to have serious anger control problems, you may risk eventually receiving the punitive responses given adults.**

Taming Your Temper: An Owner's Manual

PREDICT the FUTURE
- Watch for patterns when you lose your temper
- Watch for places where you lose your temper
- Watch for people with whom you lose your temper

STOP and THINK
- Coach yourself to make good choices
- Freeze the action so you can think
- Take as much time as you can to think before you choose

FIND CHOICES
- Think of different choices you haven't used before
- Think of lots of choices you could use
- Remember there are always lots of choices

RATE the CHOICES
- Rate the likely results of each choice
- Think about you can lose or gain with each choice
- Accurately rate the results each choice could bring

SELECT the BEST CHOICE
- Select the choice with the best likely result
- Check your choice again to be sure it's the best one
- Re-check your choice again to be sure

STICK with YOUR DECISION
- Get away from the problem
- Get away from problem people
- Get away from the area where the problem is, or could be

Resources from Youth Change

The Breakthrough Strategies to Teach and Counsel Youth Lesson Series
The pioneering lesson series that delivers powerful, problem-stopping interventions to turnaround troubled youth. These state-of-the-art strategies train unmotivated, ADHD, delinquent, special ed, oppositional, withdrawn, non-compliant and defiant youth ages 5-18, to succeed. Each book has 20 ready-to-use lessons, many with handouts.

A Child's Guide to Surviving in a Troubled Family
   Family Problems Are Never Your Fault
   Work It Out Not Act It Out ...plus 18 more lessons

Build On-the-Job Success Skills
   50 Ways to Leave Your Job— and Ever Work Again
   The Boss is Always Right ...plus 18 more lessons

Education: Don't Start the Millennium Without It
   So, Which Millennium Will You Be Ready For?
   The More You Learn, the More You Earn. ...plus 18 more lessons

Ready, Set, Go! for Independent Living
   Are You Ready for a Typical Day as an Adult?
   Seek and Detect Good Housing ...plus 18 more lessons

The Last Chance School Success Guide
   Even You Can Get Along with Teachers
   The Tassel is Worth the Hassle ...plus 18 more lessons

All-Time Favorite Lessons
   Top Ten Ways the Teacher Can't Tell You Need Help
   On Time Every Time ...plus 18 more lessons

Coping Skills Sampler
   Only You Can Deny Your Gang-Dependence
   The New, Improved Me ...plus 18 more lessons

Learning to Like the Kid in the Mirror
   So What's So Good About Me?
   Nobody's Perfect All the Time ...plus 18 more lessons

Temper and Tantrum Tamers
   Find Work Where Aggression Works
   Turn Down the Heat at Home ...plus 18 more lessons

Turn On the Turned-Off Student
   Putting Aside Problems During School
   Cure the Causes of School Flu ...plus 18 more lessons

What Every Girl Needs to Know About the Real World
   You Probably Can't Name the #1 Girls' Problem
   Staying Safe, Starting Now...plus 18 more lessons

The Quickest Kid Fixer-Uppers Series
The most answers in the least time. The books to turn to when you need concise, fast answers presented in a condensed, quick-access format. Each volume is packed with dozens of the best strategies to solve your most serious and persistent kid problems.
The Quickest Kid Fixer-Uppers Volumes 1, 2, 3 and 4

The Breakthrough Strategies Workshop on Videotape
Earn college credit or CEUs, plus get the entire, problem-solving workshop on 10 hours of videotape, complete with workbook and more than 100 reproducible handouts. The video workshop delivers hundreds of ready-to-use, must-have interventions to turnaround delinquency, violence, ADD, defiance, school failure, apathy, bad attitudes, non-compliance and more.

All the Best Answers for the Worst Kid Problems
New tricks and tips, and old, forgotten favorites are packed onto each of these problem-solving, 70 minute audio cassette tapes.
Anti-Social Youth, Maximum-Strength Motivation-Makers, Forgotten Favorite Strategies

---

Order by **PHONE** 1-800-545-5736 Toll-Free • **MAIL** 275 N. 3rd St, Woodburn, OR 97071
FAX 1-503-982-7910 • **E-MAIL** dwells@youthchg.com • **VISIT** www.youthchg.com

- ❏ Set of all 11 Breakthrough Series Books
- ❏ A Child's Guide to Surviving in a Troubled Family
- ❏ All-Time Favorite Lessons
- ❏ Build On-the-Job Success Skills
- ❏ Coping Skills Sampler
- ❏ Education: Don't Start the Millennium Without It
- ❏ Learning to Like the Kid in the Mirror
- ❏ Ready, Set, Go! for Independent Living
- ❏ Temper and Tantrum Tamers
- ❏ The Last Chance School Success Guide
- ❏ Turn On the Turned-Off Student
- ❏ What Every Girl Needs to Know About Real World
- ❏ The Quickest Kid Fixer-Uppers Volume 1
- ❏ The Quickest Kid Fixer-Uppers Volume 2
- ❏ The Quickest Kid Fixer-Uppers Volume 3
- ❏ The Quickest Kid Fixer-Uppers Volume 4
- ❏ Breakthrough Workshop on Videotape
- ❏ Anti-Social Youth/Best Answers Cassette
- ❏ Motivation-Makers/Best Answers Cassette
- ❏ Favorite Strategies/Best Answers Cassette

Books $13, Cassettes $13, Set 11 Breakthrough Series books $129, Video Set $169, PLUS tax & $7 shipping
Checks, Purchase Orders, VISA, AMEX, MasterCard Accepted

Name _____ Agency _____ Credit Card, Purch. Order# _____ Signature _____
Address _____ City _____ State _____ Zip _____ Phone _____